PROUD

PROUD
BY MICHAEL HEALEY

PLAYWRIGHTS CANADA PRESS
TORONTO

Playwrights Canada Press
202-269 Richmond St. W., Toronto, ON M5V 1X1
416.703.0013 • info@playwrightscanada.com • www.playwrightscanada.com

For production rights inquiries, please contact:
Pam Winter, Gary Goddard Agency
10 St. Mary St., #305, Toronto, ON M4Y 1P9
416-928-0299, goddard@canadafilm.com

We acknowledge the financial support of the Canada Council for the Arts, the
Ontario Arts Council, the Ontario Media Development Corporation, and the
Government of Canada through the Canada Book Fund for our publishing activities.

 Canada Council for the Arts **Conseil des Arts du Canada**  **ONTARIO ARTS COUNCIL CONSEIL DES ARTS DE L'ONTARIO**

Cover design by Avery Swartz
Book design by Blake Sproule

LIBRARY AND ARCHIVES CANADA CATALOGUING IN PUBLICATION
Healey, Michael, 1963-
        Proud / Michael Healey. -- 1st ed.

A play.
Issued also in electronic formats.
ISBN 978-1-77091-144-4

        I. Title.

PS8565.E14P76 2013   C812'.54   C2012-907928-6

First edition: February 2013
Printed and bound in Canada by Imprimerie Gauvin, Gatineau

For Morwyn Brebner

Proud was commissioned by Tarragon Theatre and first produced by Sue Edworthy and Proud Productions at the Berkeley Street Theatre Upstairs. It opened on September 22, 2012, with the following company:

The Prime Minister: Michael Healey
Jisbella Lyth: Maev Beaty
Cary Baines: Tom Barnett
Jake: Jeff Lillico

Director: Miles Potter
Set and costume designer: Gillian Gallow
Lighting designer: Kimberly Purtell
Sound designer: Lyon Smith
Stage manager: Arwen MacDonell

CHARACTERS

The Prime Minister
Jisbella Lyth
Cary Baines
Jake Lyth

"Although much of our life is rooted in the anxiety of time, in other words the fear of death, the continuity of knowledge and wisdom that has brought us here together is rooted in love, a love that is not only as strong as death, but able to cast out its fear."
—Northrop Frye

The above fades. The house light goes down and the following is projected somewhere:

This play begins shortly after the 2011 Canadian federal election. It deviates from reality in several ways, including this way: instead of the NDP winning fifty-nine seats in Quebec, those seats have gone to the Conservatives.

The above fades and is replaced by the following:

Question: Do you love this country?

"Well… I think the country has unlimited potential."
—The Right Honourable Stephen Harper

SCENE 1.

The PRIME MINISTER *walks on stage. There is applause. He waits.*

He smiles, genuinely, but without warmth. The applause dies.

PRIME MINISTER: Good afternoon. Thank you. I am moved, and humbled, to see you all here today.

More applause. He waits.

    (not unkindly) Please don't do that. Not that this isn't celebratory, this occasion, it is, after all, we had to move this meeting from our normal caucus venue to this much larger room to accommodate... all of you. And it's exciting, to be here, all together, and yes, our victory was historic, and I understand why there's a buzz in the room. A tingle. But applause is for campaigns, and, thanks be to the Canadian voter, we won't have to go through another one of them for four years.

Scattered, confused applause at this, which dies on the vine. He waits.

There's a time for that sort of thing. But now we must engage with the facts, and they are these: after successive minority governments, we have won our majority. And not just any majority, but the second-largest majority in the history of this country. We have won seats in parts of the country where, heretofore, conservative voices have been silent. Our win is nothing short of historic, as you've been reading and hearing. We have done this historic thing, however, with the smallest possible percentage of the popular vote. Analyzed correctly, we see that our support is broad, but it is thin. If our support was an iced-over pond, I couldn't in good conscience recommend we play shinny on it. And beneath that thin layer of support it is murky, and cold, and unforgiving. We fall into the frigid water of that pond, and not only might we die, but, more importantly, the hard work we have to do will be put on hold while we try to haul ourselves out, which is time-consuming, exhausting, and uncertain.

And yet, the mandate we have been given is one of change. We have been entrusted with the task of reforming our government, our finances, and our place in the world along principles we articulated clearly in the campaign, and which Canadians have seen fit to embrace. Change does not come easily in this country, however. Her Majesty's loyal opposition, though it's in disarray, will resist the change we seek at every turn. And often the press will be their willing ally in that resistance.

Those are the facts. And so, given the enormous task ahead and the myriad ways we will be challenged, how can we insure we do the maximum amount possible, as efficiently as possible, while encountering the least resistance possible?

He waits.

You will, each of you, get pulled a lot of ways now that you're here. Those of you serving on committees will have commitments to those committees. Those of you with new cabinet portfolios will have to get up to speed with your departments and begin managing the people under you. You will all have commitments to your constituents. You all have families to whom you are committed. To varying degrees.

That was a joke, but let me be clear. There is no greater commitment in your life than the one I ask you to make here today. I ask, I in fact insist, that you make a commitment here today to the reality that if any one of us forgets to exercise discipline where the nation's business is at stake, then we all suffer. It's discipline that will see this mandate carried out. Every single time in the past that my governments have faltered, it's because of a loss of this discipline. As Cary can tell you, (CARY Baines, the PRIME MINISTER's chief of staff, materializes from the gloom behind him.) nothing gets done if there's a crisis, except for work on that crisis. Therefore.

You can speak to no one about your work. No one. No friend, no acquaintance, no drunk in an airport lounge. Certainly no one in the press. None of the people who just devoted their lives to getting you elected, no one in our party machinery, no lobbyist. No loved one. Let me say that one again: you may not speak to your loved ones about whatever is stressing you here. If you have stress, if you have any concern, if you feel like you just need to chat, you have one option: come to me.

This is a wheel we are setting up, and you are all spokes, and I am the centre of the wheel. You all have direct access to me. You come to me. And no one else.

Cary?

CARY steps forward.

CARY: Now we're going to have a cocktail party, to get to know one another. The bar's over there, and it's open for forty-five minutes.

SCENE 2.

The PRIME MINISTER'S *office. The PM sits at his desk. There is an easel or whiteboard with a representation of the seating in the House of Commons on it. Tory-blue magnets cover the government side and two-thirds of the opposition bench. There are a few orange and red magnets on the far right of the opposition side; a single green magnet is at the farthest reaches of the opposition bench.*

PRIME MINISTER: Cary?

CARY: *(He steps in.)* Sir?

PRIME MINISTER: This is not good.

CARY *steps to the whiteboard.*

Do you see the problem?

CARY: Uh… Hang on.

PRIME MINISTER: My eye line. Who am I looking at?

CARY: Bill Foster?

PRIME MINISTER: Behind Foster and one to the left.

CARY: Uh… *Oh.*

PRIME MINISTER: Yes.

CARY: Tim Gunner.

PRIME MINISTER: Yes. So every time I rise to speak in the House, I have to look at the one Conservative politician who thinks it's a good idea for heroin users to get all the needles they need to use all the heroin they want.

CARY: His riding is in downtown Vancouver.

PRIME MINISTER: I'm aware.

CARY: He said it in 2006.

PRIME MINISTER: Again, I'm aware.

CARY: Prime Minister. If we move everyone in caucus who's ever done something to offend you away from your field of vision, well, there isn't enough room behind you, sir.

PRIME MINISTER: There are seventy-eight brand-new MPs in this government. Can you not put one of them directly across from me?

CARY: The bench over there is already loaded with newbies, I wanted to put a few of the experienced members in with them—

PRIME MINISTER: Not Tim Gunner.

CARY: Sir.

CARY removes the Tim Gunner magnet and hunts for another to replace him. Gunner goes to the far corner of the government side.

Carole Bing?

PRIME MINISTER: Defended the long-gun registry.

CARY: Anwar Petah?

PRIME MINISTER: Came out against going into Iraq with the Americans right after I said we should.

CARY: *(under his breath)* Ten years ago:...

PRIME MINISTER: Sorry?

CARY: No. Steve Quinn?

PRIME MINISTER: Told his hometown newspaper that I'm an autocrat.

CARY: He claims he was misquoted.

PRIME MINISTER: Still. Why is he speaking to them at all?

CARY: Uh... Roberto Calfaggio?

PRIME MINISTER: Are you kidding?

CARY: He was expressing a personal opinion. He was at his home. It was a cocktail party. Some journalist overheard him. It was, like, 1998!

PRIME MINISTER: Are you defending him?

CARY: No! But there's nobody else to put over there that's spent any time in the House.

PRIME MINISTER: Then fill it with new people. I'll keep an eye on them.

CARY: But... okay.

CARY shuffles magnets. The PRIME MINISTER returns to his desk. JISBELLA Lyth, thirty-five, comes through the door. She's a little breathless.

JISBELLA: Hi!

PRIME MINISTER: Hello.

JISBELLA: Either of you guys got a condom?

There is a pause.

I got a guy in my new office and he wants to christen it with me.

A beat.

I'm the new member for Cormier–Lac-Poule.

PRIME MINISTER: Yes. Ms.... Lyth, is it?

JISBELLA: Jisbella Lyth. We met last week. At a thing in the riding.

PRIME MINISTER: Yes. Ms. Lyth.

JISBELLA: Call me Jisbella. Or Bella.

PRIME MINISTER: Yes. Okay.

JISBELLA: Call me Jis if you want.

PRIME MINISTER: I most certainly will not.

JISBELLA: Yeah. That's more of a back-home thing. So? Condom? Sir?

CARY: Is there something I can do for you, Ms. Lyth?

JISBELLA: It's a weird ask, I know, but let's face it, it's a weird day! I haven't got any staff yet, and I was gonna make some calls, but I was just sitting there in my office, and I'm like: This is my office! My parliamentary office! I'm an MP! And, like, I'm sitting there, stunned, and in walks this guy and he starts asking me questions.

CARY: What guy?

PRIME MINISTER: *(simultaneous)* What guy is that?

JISBELLA: Well, now I can't remember his name. Eric? Something like that.

PRIME MINISTER: Is he press?

JISBELLA: I think so. He said he works for CBC. Anyway, I show him my new desk, and then we're making out, and I'm like, "Do you have a condom?" and he's like, "I used to, but the campaign was really intense, and now I can't expense any more until the beginning of next month," blah blah, like, this guy loves to talk, right? So—

PRIME MINISTER: Curly hair?

JISBELLA: Yes!

PRIME MINISTER: Evan? Is that his name?

JISBELLA: Yes! Thank you. *Evan.*

CARY: She's about to have sex with Evan Solomon.

PRIME MINISTER: On her desk.

JISBELLA: Not unless someone has a condom!

A beat.

You said we should come straight to you if we needed anything.

PRIME MINISTER: I also said you shouldn't be speaking to anyone.

JISBELLA: This is the genius of my strategy. If we're doing it, he's not asking me questions. I hope.

PRIME MINISTER: That's a tactic, not a strategy.

JISBELLA: Really?

PRIME MINISTER: Yes.

JISBELLA: Interesting. Clearly, I have much to learn. Anyhoo.

She waits.

Oh! Oh!! Have I offended you? Your religion? Do you not believe in condoms?

PRIME MINISTER: No, I…

JISBELLA: Some of us were talking earlier about that. About your secret religion.

PRIME MINISTER: Were you?

JISBELLA: Yes. Nobody knows what religion you are. Someone said you were a, like a Christian Scientist.

PRIME MINISTER: Did they.

JISBELLA: Not a Christian Scientist, one of the other freaky ones.

PRIME MINISTER: Who were you speaking to about this?

JISBELLA: One of our guys at the party. Tall guy? Skinny? Weird beard?

The PRIME MINISTER *and* CARY *share a look.* CARY *exiles a magnet to the back bench.*

By the way, that was the worst party I've ever seen. Two-beer maximum? The whole thing over after a half-hour? I think I can be useful, sir, as maybe the person who organizes parties for the party from here on out. Like, party planning is a strength I feel I can bring to the party. You don't mind, do you, Harry?

CARY: It's Cary.

JISBELLA: Jesus! I've met a hundred people today! And so many at the place, the riding! I had no idea. Anyway, sorry. I'm gonna be fucked for names for a little while, but then, once they go in, they stay in for life. Which reminds me: Who am I about to have sex with?

PRIME MINISTER: Evan Solomon.

JISBELLA: Evan, Evan, Evan. Okay. So? No condoms in here, is the feeling I'm getting, am I right?

CARY: Come with me, Ms. Lyth.

JISBELLA: I mean it, call me Jisbella.

CARY: Come with me, Jisbella.

PRIME MINISTER: Actually, Ms. Lyth, stay here, if you would. Cary, will you go and get the template?

CARY: Really? First day? It's a nice little honeymoon we're having here.

PRIME MINISTER: We've seen in the past that getting personnel news out of the way early saves us trouble later.

CARY: Yes.

He goes. There is a pause.

PRIME MINISTER: I appointed someone unelected to cabinet once. I gave
    him a Senate seat. Another time, I talked a Liberal into becoming
    a Conservative days after his constituents elected him as a Liberal.
    I did both these things right at the start of a mandate. Get the bad
    news out early, Ms. Lyth. That's a strategy.

JISBELLA: Right on.

A pause.

What's he going to get? Not condoms?

PRIME MINISTER: No. Not condoms. He's going to get a resignation letter.

JISBELLA: Who's resigning?

PRIME MINISTER: You are.

A beat.

I have a friend, a former friend, who wrote a book called *Game
Theory and Canadian Politics.* What you want, he said, is a majority
that's big enough so you get your way, but not too big. A majority
that's too large is unstable. So. You get to be first off the plank.

JISBELLA: You're firing me?

PRIME MINISTER: You're going to resign. You can sit as an independent.
    I'm just moving you from here *(He's at the board, indicating her seat in
    parliament.)* all the way over here *(He moves her magnet to the far corner
    of the opposition benches).* You can chat with Elizabeth May.

JISBELLA: You're firing me because I asked you for a condom?

PRIME MINISTER: Because you show spectacularly bad judgment, and also because it's in my interest to do so. We were too successful in this election. You're helping me out.

JISBELLA: That's so unfair. You said to come to you. I'M JUST TRYING TO HAVE SEX WITH THAT GUY!

PRIME MINISTER: Nonetheless.

JISBELLA: I won't resign.

PRIME MINISTER: Yes you will. I have a file on each of my rookie MPs. Cary will bring yours in. Your file contains personal details about you that I can use as leverage, if need be.

JISBELLA: I haven't done anything.

PRIME MINISTER: I'm not interested in curbing your appetites in any way. I only ask that you indulge them outside the Conservative Party of Canada.

JISBELLA: You fucking prick!

PRIME MINISTER: And that's the first time anyone's called me that.

CARY *comes back with a file.*

JISBELLA: Hey! Gary!

CARY: Cary.

JISBELLA: Who gives a fuck. What's a rotten borough?

CARY: I beg your pardon?

JISBELLA: What's a rotten borough?

CARY: It's—

PRIME MINISTER: It's a riding where you can run whatever candidate you like, qualified or not, because they have no hope of winning.

JISBELLA: I ran because I was told there was no way I'd win. Cormier–Lac-Poule was supposed to be a rotten borough.

PRIME MINISTER: The magnitude of our win took everyone by surprise.

JISBELLA: So here's the thing. It's possible that I was not in the riding the day my nomination papers were signed.

A pause.

PRIME MINISTER: Really.

JISBELLA: In fact, I guess I have proof I wasn't there.

PRIME MINISTER: I see.

JISBELLA: Photographic proof. I was in Cancun.

CARY: You're telling us you committed some sort of election fraud?

PRIME MINISTER: No. She's telling us we did. Someone from the party signed her nomination papers. And paid off whoever accepted them.

JISBELLA: Is that what I'm saying?

A pause.

PRIME MINISTER: Cary, we won't be needing the resignation letter. Ms. Lyth, the minister of defence will have condoms in his office.

JISBELLA: Thank you.

PRIME MINISTER: But they may not be the right size.

She strides out.

CARY: I'll figure out how to bury her nomination. We can at least raise doubts about her credibility if she goes public with the fraud story.

PRIME MINISTER: That's okay.

CARY: What?

PRIME MINISTER: That's okay. Leave it alone.

CARY starts to leave.

Leave the file, will you?

CARY drops the file on the desk and goes. The PRIME MINISTER regards it. As the lights fade he opens the file, sits, and reads.

Blackout.

SCENE 3.

JISBELLA sits. The PRIME MINISTER stands.

PRIME MINISTER: Strategy: strategy is long-term thinking about how to achieve goals.

JISBELLA: Yes.

PRIME MINISTER: A tactic is an act you take in the short term that serves a particular strategy.

JISBELLA: Okay.

PRIME MINISTER: It always bugs me when people confuse the two.

JISBELLA: I bet. Can I get a coffee?

PRIME MINISTER: No.

JISBELLA: You have a coffee.

PRIME MINISTER: I do. Now—

JISBELLA: What time is it? I mean, holy shit.

PRIME MINISTER: Now. There are certain things the press pays attention to and certain things they don't. Sometimes we have a little trouble figuring out which things they're going to pick up on and which things they are going to ignore.

JISBELLA: That must drive you nuts.

PRIME MINISTER: The long-form census is an example of this. We thought we could kill it without the press noticing. Turns out they noticed. That took us by surprise.

JISBELLA: The long-form... what?

PRIME MINISTER: Never mind. I'm trying to make a point.

JISBELLA: Go ahead. Can I just get a coffee?

PRIME MINISTER: Absolutely not. So, in looking ahead, there are programs I want to enact, programs that I feel might raise the ire of the press, and I want to do what I can to minimize that. So—

JISBELLA's phone rings.

JISBELLA: Hang on.

(She picks up.) Hey! Good morning, mister! How are you? I had to sneak out before you woke up.

Because I have a meeting with an old, crazy person. He's right here, do you want to say hello? Okay.

(She hands the PM the phone.) It's my son. He wants to say hello.

PRIME MINISTER: *(taking the phone)* Hello. Is this—

Yes, sorry your mum had to come in early. I—

No. No, I don't. Do you want to ask your mother? Okay. Bye.

(handing the phone back) He wants to know how to make a latke.

JISBELLA: You want a latke for breakfast? Are you crazy? Have some cereal like a normal person.

What do you mean there's no cereal?

Oh, right, okay.

Okay, okay: take a potato—

The PRIME MINSTER rolls his eyes, sits.

—and take the grater. Grate the potato. Squeeze out the water, then grate a bit of onion in there too.

I don't know, a bit. Peel the onion first. Then, you know where the breadcrumbs are? Take a handful of breadcrumbs, mix it all together. Put oil in the pan, get it nice and hot, and CAREFULLY put the latke in the oil. Flip it when the edge is brown. That's it. Is there applesauce? Okay. You got it? Good. Don't make a mess. Call me back before you leave for school.

Because it's a new school and I need to make sure you remember how to get there.

Okay.

Okay. I love you too. Enjoy that latke.

She hangs up. A beat.

PRIME MINISTER: Your son is how old?

JISBELLA: Jake is seven. What did he say to you?

PRIME MINISTER: Is he alone?

JISBELLA: He better be. He loves to cook. Where were we? How's your coffee.

(rising) Can I get you another—?

PRIME MINISTER: No. So the strategy is: I want to make sure the press doesn't focus on the thing that I'm going to do.

JISBELLA: What are you going to do?

PRIME MINISTER: The first thing I'm going to do is reform the PCO. The Privy Council Office. Under the Liberals the number of people working there ballooned. I'm going to shrink it again.

JISBELLA: Why?

PRIME MINISTER: It doesn't need to be that big. Also, there are people there who were appointed by the Liberals and remain loyal to the Liberals. It's so petty. The PCO loved us at the beginning.

JISBELLA: They did?

PRIME MINISTER: Oh yeah. When we came in, in 2006, as a minority, we had a narrow agenda focused on five priorities. Remember?

JISBELLA: No.

PRIME MINISTER: No?

JISBELLA: No.

PRIME MINISTER: You don't remember, when we got elected in 2006, how we focused on five things?

JISBELLA: Really?

PRIME MINISTER: Did you notice the GST went down?

JISBELLA: The GST went down?

PRIME MINISTER: I mean, really?

JISBELLA: I was fucking busy in 2006. The GST went down?

PRIME MINISTER: The point is, the PCO loved us when we came in because we had five things to do and it was easy for them to plan and get things done.

JISBELLA: Sure.

PRIME MINISTER: But now I'm going to trim them, and they aren't going to like it.

JISBELLA: Trim them by how much?

PRIME MINISTER: Nearly a third. And I need your help with that.

JISBELLA: Righto. You want me to go fire some people? I've never done that before.

PRIME MINISTER: No.

JISBELLA: Well, I fired a dishwasher at the restaurant that I was manager of, but, really, all that meant was, like, he wasn't showing up for his shifts, so—

PRIME MINISTER: Ms. Lyth…

JISBELLA: —like, at all, so I called him and got his machine, and so—

PRIME MINISTER: Ms. Lyth…

JISBELLA: I called this guy—

PRIME MINISTER: I don't care.

JISBELLA: I'M TALKING. I CARE.

A beat.

> And I just got his machine so I fired him over his machine. I'm not sure if that counts.

PRIME MINISTER: I don't want you to fire people. I want you to distract the press.

JISBELLA: Okay.

PRIME MINISTER: So, in a couple weeks' time, you're going to stand up in parliament and introduce a private member's bill.

JISBELLA: Okay.

A beat.

PRIME MINISTER: Don't you want to know what's in the bill?

JISBELLA: That coffee you've got smells like ass. And yet I still want some. Can I have just a sip?

PRIME MINISTER: Yes, here, take the coffee.

JISBELLA: Thanks.

PRIME MINISTER: God.

She drinks.

JISBELLA: You're the fucking prime minister of Canada. And this is what you drink in the morning?

PRIME MINISTER: It's decaf.

JISBELLA: *(handing it back)* You sick motherfu—

PRIME MINISTER: You're going to introduce a bill limiting abortion.

JISBELLA: An anti-abortion bill?

PRIME MINISTER: A pro-life bill. Cary will draft it for you. I will pretend to be caught off guard. I'll say that you're acting on your own and that I strongly disapprove. The press will spend several days gleefully watching your rebellion, I'll cut the PCO down to size, and they will miss the story.

JISBELLA: And what happens to the bill?

PRIME MINISTER: If it ever comes to a vote, it'll be defeated. And you'll have a reputation as a maverick. You'll be the thorn in my side, Ms. Lyth. Every time we need to do something difficult, we'll make sure you're doing something stupid at the same moment. Okay?

JISBELLA: You know, I've had an abortion.

PRIME MINISTER: You've had two.

JISBELLA: *(a beat)* That's right.

PRIME MINISTER: That will come out at some point. We'll leak it if we have to.

A pause.

JISBELLA: Okay.

PRIME MINISTER: Okay?

JISBELLA: Okay.

A beat.

PRIME MINISTER: Any questions?

JISBELLA: No, I got it.

PRIME MINISTER: There will be a kind of intense scrutiny for a while.

JISBELLA: Sure.

PRIME MINISTER: Just be yourself. Tell people whatever you feel.

JISBELLA: As long as it's anti-abortion, right?

PRIME MINISTER: Pro-life, yes.

JISBELLA: Can I say it bugs the shit out of me that people say pro-life when they mean anti-abortion?

PRIME MINISTER: Sure.

A pause. He's looking at her.

JISBELLA: What?

PRIME MINISTER: You don't have a problem doing this? Morally?

JISBELLA: Nope.

PRIME MINISTER: But, I mean, I assume you're pro-abortion.

JISBELLA: Pro-choice you mean. Who says I believe in anything?

PRIME MINISTER: I see. But...

JISBELLA: Yes?

PRIME MINISTER: No.

A pause.

That's too bad.

JISBELLA: What is?

PRIME MINISTER: Well, I had assumed you were going to object to the plan. I...

JISBELLA: Yes?

PRIME MINISTER: No, nothing. I had come up with several compelling arguments, that's all.

JISBELLA: Really.

PRIME MINISTER: Yes. Never mind. Okay.

JISBELLA: You were going to change my mind? On abortion?

PRIME MINISTER: Yes.

JISBELLA: Using some arguments?

PRIME MINISTER: It's, never mind.

JISBELLA: Well, now I would like to hear those amazing arguments. Because they sound like they would be amazing.

PRIME MINISTER: Well, sorry. Now I don't need to deploy them.

JISBELLA: Fuck! I was too easy! But what if your arguments didn't work?

PRIME MINISTER: Oh, they would have worked.

JISBELLA: I'm sure. But what if they hadn't?

PRIME MINISTER: In that case... I was going to flirt with you.

A beat. She's dumbstruck.

JISBELLA: You were going to try arguments... and then flirting?

PRIME MINISTER: I was going to, yes, in a way, flirt with you. My sense is that you respond to flirtatious behaviour.

JISBELLA: That's your sense?

PRIME MINISTER: That's my read, yes. Am I wrong?

JISBELLA: No. In fact, next time skip the arguments and go straight for the flirting. Because I'm dying to see that shit.

A pause.

PRIME MINISTER: So, this is troubling. You have no beliefs? At all?

JISBELLA: I wouldn't say that. I have beliefs.

PRIME MINISTER: Can you tell me what they are?

JISBELLA: Not at six fucking thirty in the morning without coffee I can't.

CARY comes in with a large coffee.

CARY: Here you go.

JISBELLA: Jesus! Where the fuck did you come from?

CARY: I was listening. Black two sugars, right?

JISBELLA: You were listening?

CARY: I just felt like understanding you, who you are, would be useful in the project we are starting here. I think the thorn-in-the-side idea's a good one, and you seem like the person for the job, so, I just was hoping to get a sense of who you are, Jisbella.

The PM is laughing.

JISBELLA: What's funny?

PRIME MINISTER: Don't let Cary fool you. He was hoping to hear something he can use against you.

JISBELLA: Really? Is that true?

CARY: *(a little blush)* Yes. I find that generally when people start by talking about their beliefs, they wind up saying some very personal things. Which can be then used against them, if need be.

JISBELLA: Are you going to tell him to fuck off?

PRIME MINISTER: Why?

A beat.

JISBELLA: Okay. It's fun around here. You want beliefs?

PRIME MINISTER: If you've got them, sure.

CARY: Yes please.

JISBELLA: Okay. Let me see…

> I believe education makes half the people in it feel stupid. I believe
> you should have to get a licence to be a parent the way you need
> one to drive a car. I believe your first impression of a person is al-
> ways wrong. I believe everyone is snob. About something. And the
> worst snobs are the people that say they aren't snobs about anything.
> Should you be writing this down?

CARY: I'm good.

JISBELLA: Uh… I believe no one respects single mothers. Including single
mothers. I believe that religion is weird, fucked up, and stupid because it's made by people that are weird, fucked up, and stupid. Sorry.

PRIME MINISTER: No no.

JISBELLA: What else? I believe the government is a good place for a
government job, and that's basically the only thing going for it. I
believe most men hate women, but that's okay because most men
hate men, and most women hate themselves.

PRIME MINISTER: Really?

JISBELLA: Really. What else? Dogs are awesome, cats are stupid. Dog people are awesome and cat people are stupid. Men only help women
for one reason, and that reason rhymes with "pussy." Uh… oh! I
believe the pension I'm gonna get for being an MP is stupid.

PRIME MINISTER: You can always kick it back if you think you don't deserve it.

JISBELLA: Oh, I'll keep it. You're dumb enough to give it to me. But if I last here for six years, the pension I'll get for the rest of my life is more than I made being the manager at St-Hubert. It's disgusting. I worked fucking hard at that stupid job, the best job I could get. And now I'm here doing I don't know what, running some sort of abortion scam I guess, and I get free money for the rest of my life.

It's fucked up, and I'll totally take it.

CARY: Morally casual. She's a Jenny.

PRIME MINISTER: Mostly a Jenny. But there's a strong Dougie streak in her.

CARY: The anger, yes. Total Dougie. Maybe even a bit of Clive.

PRIME MINISTER: No, not Clive. No sense of superiority.

CARY: No, I just meant the anger is nearly Clive-ian in its certainty.

PRIME MINISTER: True. But the essentially unexamined entitlement excludes any Clive. She's a Jenny–Dougie.

CARY: Weird. Not a hybrid we ever encountered.

PRIME MINISTER: It's true.

(to her) A couple of elections ago, we divided up the population into recognizable types and gave them names. That way we could decide which groups to go after for their support and which groups to ignore because they'd never support us.

CARY: And you straddle two of those groups. One of which would never support us—the Jenny part of you—because you distrust men and have vague, unexamined progressive politics. But you also have a working-class love of fairness and a desire for moral simplicity.

PRIME MINISTER: As long as that simplicity isn't applied to you. Just the world around you. That's the Dougie part.

JISBELLA: This is how you spend your time?

CARY: This is how we got this far.

PRIME MINISTER: We got very good at marketing to people that weren't being marketed to.

JISBELLA: Convincing people that you believe whatever they believe.

PRIME MINISTER: That's the thing. The vast majority of people don't have beliefs. They have feelings, vague ideas that flow from those feelings, but they don't have actual beliefs.

CARY: That list of things you gave us?

JISBELLA: Yeah?

CARY: Not actually beliefs.

JISBELLA: Fuck you!

CARY: You can tell because it's all negatively expressed: this is stupid, this is wrong, that's a shitty thing I hate. When we realized that's how people respond when you actually listen to them, we became masters at channelling those feelings.

JISBELLA: You're saying I don't believe the things I believe? That nobody does?

PRIME MINISTER: We're saying that beliefs are such an academic exercise that most people don't bother with them. Your feelings are what guide you. But I wonder, now that she's here and doing this, if she shouldn't—

CARY: I was gonna suggest the same thing—

Her phone rings. As she reaches for it:

JISBELLA: Oh! Shit!

CARY: What?

JISBELLA: I forgot the egg!

She answers.

Sweetie! I forgot to tell you to mix in an egg! I'm sorry. How is the latke?

Yeah. I thought so. It's pretty shitty without the egg. Well, don't cry! I'm sorry. It's my fault. Don't cry. Sweetie. Sweetie? Ohhh.

She's at a loss. The PRIME MINISTER gestures for the phone.

PRIME MINISTER: Hey. Is that Jake? Hey, Jake. It's okay. It's okay. I know. It's not a latke. But you know what, Jake? That's some motherfreakin' hash browns you got there. Uh huh. Hash browns. Jake: you go into any man's diner or truck stop across the country, and you know what they give you with your eggs? Motherfreakin' hash browns, that's right. And you know what? I wish I was there to eat them with you, because those hash browns smell good. Because I can smell them through the motherfreakin' phone, that's how good they smell. Now you put away that stupid applesauce, get some ketchup, and you enjoy those hash browns, okay? Okay. Bye-bye.

Gives her the phone.

JISBELLA: Sweetie? Ketchup's in the… oh, you know where the motherfreakin' ketchup is, do you? Okay then. Talk to you soo—.

Nice. Thanks.

PRIME MINISTER: Don't mention it. Now. I want you to do something for me.

JISBELLA: Okay.

PRIME MINISTER: You're a politician now. Figure out what your beliefs are and get back to me. Just as an exercise. Express them as positives, and make them about the country, or at least about society.

JISBELLA: Okay. I'm doing this why?

PRIME MINISTER: Just, you know, for fun.

JISBELLA: Fun. Right.

CARY: You're unique. A rare hybrid. It'll be useful.

PRIME MINISTER: But also: I'm turning you into one of us. A member of the political class.

A beat, then the PRIME MINISTER emits a ghoulish laugh. There is an embarrassed silence. He shrugs.

Blackout.

SCENE 3A.

JAKE, twenty-five, enters. There is a chair. He notices an earpiece on the chair. He puts it in.

JAKE: Hello?

Hi.

Yes I can.

Okay.

He takes a body mic from the chair and puts it under his shirt, snaking it up and attaching it to his collar. He sits.

Yes. How's this?

Uh, what should I... I'm happy to be here today. I'm, I'm very happy to be here today. I'm happy to be—okay.

A pause.

Sorry? No. It rhymes with "myth."

No problem.

Okay. I will.

He waits. The lights fade on him.

Blackout.

SCENE 4.

The office is empty for a moment. Then CARY *and* JISBELLA *rush in;* CARY *slams the door.*

JISBELLA: Well, that was fucking fun.

CARY: Could you feel all the air go out of the House of Commons when you introduced the bill?

JISBELLA: You didn't tell me that was going to be so much fun.

CARY: The first time the word "abortion" came out of your mouth, it was like—

JISBELLA: It was like you could hear every anus in the room slamming shut.

CARY: I like the way you glanced up and smiled when the hush fell on the House. That'll be on every channel tonight.

JISBELLA: Fucking awesome.

CARY: You are.

A beat between them. She's exhilarated.

JISBELLA: I looked at the talking points you gave me. Am I really supposed to say that I'm doing this because my constituents want it?

CARY: Yes.

JISBELLA: Do they?

CARY: We did some polling. There are some in your riding that want this.

JISBELLA: How many is some?

CARY: The number doesn't matter. The point is, when you call people up and tell them that this is the only country without any regulation whatsoever on abortion, people will say they want a law of some kind.

JISBELLA: I guess you can always find the poll results you're looking for.

CARY: That's just being professional. But the cool thing is this: if you can keep someone on the phone for more than thirty seconds, their brain is yours for the taking.

JISBELLA: Really.

CARY: It's how we became the best fundraisers on the planet. We revolutionized the process. We don't count on corporate donations; our money comes in twenties and fifties. You know how you do that? You just get people on the phone, get them talking. You just shut up and let them go. Every other party, when they do their fundraising, there's a script the caller has to get through—here's what we did, here's what we're gonna do, how much can you give. But when our people call, they ask you one question then just shut up. It's awesome to watch.

JISBELLA: What's the question?

CARY: Some variation on "Tell me: just how pissed off are you?"

JISBELLA: You ask people to complain?

CARY: We ask them to give us their feelings. Politics is fundamentally an emotional event. The reason you're so valuable to us is because you have direct access to your emotions. People hear you speak, they know you're actually feeling something. That's why there are no stats in your talking points. They're just pure emotion: some law is better than no law when people's *lives are at stake*, reopening the debate is the *honest* thing to do, Canadians *feel* having no regulation on this issue is *crazy*.

JISBELLA: And I have a *moral obligation* to listen to the anti-abortion *nutbars* back home who have *begged me* to do this.

CARY: Yes.

JISBELLA: Super.

A beat.

CARY: It'll all be over in a bit. You will eventually withdraw the bill. And then he'll give you a committee to run or make you someone's parliamentary secretary. This is a huge opportunity.

The PRIME MINISTER *enters, closing the door.*

PRIME MINISTER: Way to go. I've got a few journalists hanging around out in the hall. Ready?

JISBELLA: Uh huh.

PRIME MINISTER: *(opening the door, shouting)* Goddamn it, Ms. Lyth! Private members' bills are supposed to get approval through this office before you stand up in the House and make a spectacle of yourself!

A beat while he waits for her to respond.

JISBELLA: I don't give a shit! My constituents *feel* this is too important!

PRIME MINISTER: You don't seem to understand how we do things here!

JISBELLA: I don't give a shit how *you* do things, I'm doing the *moral* thing!

PRIME MINISTER: There are procedures, okay? I understand you want to make a name for your—

JISBELLA: And I understand that you're a fucking pussy! Well FUCK YOU! I'M DOING THIS FOR THE PEOPLE THAT ELECTED ME, YOU WISHY-WASHY, NON-UTERUS-HAVING CUNT WITH A HAIRCUT!

A moment of stunned silence at her tirade, then the PM turns on CARY.

PRIME MINISTER: And you, assbox. What's your excuse? She has to give the Speaker forty-eight hours' notice. How come nobody figured out she was going to do this? Huh? HUH?

CARY: *(faux-cowed)* I don't know.

PRIME MINISTER: You don't know. You don't know. That's just great!

The PRIME MINISTER kicks over a chair. It takes two tries.

You know, from the first day I hired you I knew you were gonna fuck me somehow.

CARY: *(laughing)* I know. I know. I…

PRIME MINISTER: You make me sick!

CARY: *(He's laughing too hard.)* Okay.

PRIME MINISTER: Get the fuck out of my—

(but now he's laughing) Aw, fuck it. Stay in here so I can yell at you some more.

He slams the door shut. A beat of recovery.

> And tomorrow I'll deny we fought, and then it's a two-day story. And then you admit we fought, and so on and so forth. So. How'd it feel to stand up in parliament and table an honest-to-God bill?

JISBELLA: I finally understand why you guys think what goes on down there is important. It actually feels important.

PRIME MINISTER: You did a great job. Ready to talk to the press about it?

JISBELLA: Cary's been prepping me.

PRIME MINISTER: That's good. But don't worry too much about the talking points. Just get out there and let loose.

JISBELLA: What if I say something wrong?

PRIME MINISTER: Nothing you can say hurts us.

CARY: You have a very appealing guilelessness.

JISBELLA: You mean I'm stupid.

CARY: I mean you're appealingly stupid.

JISBELLA: I still don't know why you didn't use someone who actually believes in an abortion bill.

PRIME MINISTER: Because those guys and their beliefs are exhausting to be around. But… we never had the conversation about what *your* beliefs are.

JISBELLA: Oh yeah!

CARY: Maybe we should save that and get her out in front of the press.

PRIME MINISTER: Let 'em wait. So? Have you got some beliefs for me?

JISBELLA: I did better than that. I figured out why they're a waste of time.

She dives into her purse, comes up with a few ragged pages.

PRIME MINISTER: Oh ho!

JISBELLA: Yeah. Tell me: Why is proportional representation such a great idea?

PRIME MINISTER: It's not. It's a terrible idea.

JISBELLA: You used to love it. How do you feel about access to information?

PRIME MINISTER: Also terrible.

JISBELLA: You once said that without it, quote, "…incompetent governance can be hidden under a cloak of secrecy."

CARY: Well, of course.

PRIME MINISTER: We weren't in power yet. Look, is this your point? That because my views on certain things have changed over the course of my career there's no reason for you to hold any core beliefs?

JISBELLA: Coalition with separatists.

PRIME MINISTER: Yes. A great idea when I was pursuing it, treason when they wanted to do it.

JISBELLA: Transparent government.

CARY: You ran on that in 2006.

PRIME MINISTER: As one does. Anything else?

JISBELLA: Quebec: no special status? Or is it a "nation within Canada"?

PRIME MINISTER: Whichever one works for you. Because these things, these inconsistencies, they're just situational. They have nothing to do with what I believe.

JISBELLA: Do you believe in having integrity?

CARY: Oh ho!

PRIME MINISTER: I have an enormous amount of integrity. And I keep it as far from this building as possible.

CARY: And integrity is the last thing Canadians want in their politicians. It's like the environment. Voters say they want it until you tell them what it's gonna cost.

PRIME MINISTER: One more time: things I say, the positions I take, the strategies I employ—these are all tools to acquire power. Beliefs are what you serve when you have it. You'd better figure out what you believe, because I'm going to give you a little power sometime soon. And you have to know how you want to use it, or it'll use you.

CARY: You'd better go. Ben's got hockey.

PRIME MINISTER: Yes. I'll make a few awkward statements, then I'll duck out.

He turns, then stops.

Oh, by the way. Do you have a car you'd be willing to crash?

JISBELLA: No.

PRIME MINISTER: Too bad. We're making some changes to the Environmental Assessment Act.

CARY: We're streamlining the process.

JISBELLA: That sounds good.

PRIME MINISTER: Well, yes, we're also changing the rules so that even if a project completely fails its environmental assessment, cabinet can still okay the project. Which is going to be… funky. I was thinking you could wreck your car the day that comes out.

JISBELLA: I don't drive. Sorry.

CARY: Are you sleeping with anyone at the moment?

JISBELLA is about to respond.

PRIME MINISTER: For God's sake, don't tell me. But that's a good idea, maybe you could make out with him in a restaurant or something. Anyway, we've got a couple of weeks. Think about it.

(to CARY) Who's Ben playing?

CARY: They're playing Walt's Outdoor Products. Peggy Nash's son is on that team, Jonathan. He plays right wing.

PRIME MINISTER: Great. I want to get Peggy's take on the Greek debt crisis.

The PRIME MINISTER goes.

CARY: Oh, poor Peggy.

JISBELLA: He wants to ask the NDP finance critic about Greece?

CARY: He'll talk to anyone about this stuff. Seriously, don't ever show any interest in economics when he's around.

JISBELLA: No problem.

CARY: I mean it, he started talking to me once about Hayek's concept for the denationalization of money as we boarded a plane in Belarus. The only reason he stopped was because the limo pulled in front of his house. When I got home, I realized I had pooped my shorts a little. He literally bored the shit out of me.

JISBELLA: You like him.

CARY: I admire him more than any politician I've ever met.

A beat.

Which is going to make it really hard to leave this job.

JISBELLA: Wait. When are you leaving? Did he fire you?

CARY: No, but it's only a matter of time. I'll fuck something up, or he'll need me to take one for the team during some shitstorm. That's why there's so much turnover in this job. Being chief of staff is like getting handed a grenade—it's gonna go off at some point.

JISBELLA: Uh huh.

CARY: So, *are* you sleeping with anyone at the moment?

The question hangs between them as the lights fade.

Blackout.

SCENE 5.

It's late, and the PRIME MINISTER *sits at his desk, reading.* JISBELLA *enters. She stands still until he closes the file he's reading.*

JISBELLA: I'm sitting in the car. I don't know how old I am. I think I'm...
I don't know. I'm small. I don't know where my brother is or my
sisters. I'm sitting in the car with my dad. We are parked in front of
my aunt's house. My mom is in there. My mom is staying in that
house. I don't know why. Well, to get away from us. That was why.
She needed to get away from us. She—

PRIME MINISTER: What are you doing?

JISBELLA: I'm telling you what I believe.

I don't know how old I am. He says: Stay in here. He says: I'll be
back in five minutes. He gets out.

A pause.

How am I supposed to know how long five minutes is?

PRIME MINISTER: Do you want to sit down?

JISBELLA: I'm alone. I'm alone for too long. I get out, I'm knocking on
the door, ringing the bell, nothing's happening. I can hear them
in there. But nobody comes. And now, there's this neighbour lady
suddenly standing there, she's trying to find out who I am. I can't
tell her 'cause I'm crying. She's asking me and I can't tell her, I don't
want to tell her, because then I would have to say: My father left me
in the car and my mother doesn't want me.

PRIME MINISTER: Sit down.

JISBELLA: What I believe in is myself.

> The only thing a person can rely on, or should rely on, is herself. You are the only one that knows what's right for you, and you should never give that power up to anyone else.

PRIME MINISTER: I agree.

JISBELLA: You do?

PRIME MINISTER: Sit down.

JISBELLA sits. A pause.

JISBELLA: Sorry.

PRIME MINISTER: No.

JISBELLA: It's embarrassing.

PRIME MINISTER: Why?

JISBELLA: You didn't ask for my life story. You asked what I believe in.

PRIME MINISTER: There's no difference. Would you like a drink?

JISBELLA: Uh…

Her cellphone rings.

> Hey. Are you still up? What are you doing?

> Uh huh.

Best score tonight?

Not bad. Best word?

U–what?

Utricle. Utricle. I don't even know what that—

PRIME MINISTER: Little sac of fluid in your ear.

JISBELLA: It's a little sac in your ear. Speaking of which: You take a bath?

PRIME MINISTER: *(to himself)* It orients you. Keeps you on your feet.

JISBELLA: What are you waiting for? You were supposed to be in bed an hour ago.

I know. I know, I know. I'm sorry. I can't. I can't. Because. I'm here, okay. Bathe, okay? Jakie? Just take a bath. Then go to bed. I'll be there when you wake up. In fact…

I just found out that tomorrow is take-your-kid-to-work day around here.

Uh huh. You get the day off school, and you can come here with me.

I don't know, we'll do something. Well, yes, I'm told there *is* a library here. That's what you want to do? We're not doing that. No. Listen, there's a restaurant here, we can sit there all day and eat the world's worst french fries. It'll be fun. Well, sure, if he's around you can meet him. Okay? Okay. Bathe and go to bed, mister.

I love you.

Well, you better.

She hangs up.

PRIME MINISTER: I'm pretty sure I can find some time for him.

JISBELLA: Oh no, that's okay. He wants to meet John Baird.

PRIME MINISTER: Really?

JISBELLA: He says John Baird has a baby head. On a grown-up body. He's fascinated by it.

PRIME MINISTER: Fair enough.

There is a pause between them.

JISBELLA: So…

PRIME MINISTER: It's funny: I have a story like yours, to some extent. My father's father was a respected man in Halifax, a high-school principal, a community leader. We all loved and admired him. And one day he just disappeared. They never found him, he never returned. After five years, he was declared legally dead. And that… was weird. I mean, obviously, but. I learned that your family is not inevitable. I learned that the only inevitable thing is: you.

That realization—it hurt at the time. But there's great strength in it: each day, I am for me. It doesn't preclude others, it makes others seem more real. It makes love possible, because once you recognize how truly alone we are, it makes the possibility of our coming together a concrete thing. Would you like a drink?

JISBELLA: Sure, I'll have a drink.

He crosses to the credenza, finds Scotch, pours two glasses.

PRIME MINISTER: So now that you've identified your belief, self-reliance, what do you want to do with it?

JISBELLA: No idea. I mean, we make laws. Laws control people. The thing I apparently believe in is the exact opposite of that.

PRIME MINISTER: Strauss, Hayek, even Keynes to some extent struggled with that huge question.

JISBELLA: Are they those weird-looking guys from New Brunswick? Always eating together?

PRIME MINISTER: A philosopher and two economists. They were all interested in discovering what role governments played in personal freedom.

JISBELLA: Government is the opposite of personal freedom, isn't it?

PRIME MINISTER: Actually, helping people become self-reliant is one of the things a government can do best. The central conversation of all Western democracies is: How do you make the people as free as possible?

JISBELLA: How about by just *leaving them alone*? Isn't that the definition of freedom?

PRIME MINISTER: No, that's the definition of loneliness. Have you had a hamburger lately?

JISBELLA: Um, yeah, at lunch. Fries were terrible.

PRIME MINISTER: Did you die after you ate that hamburger?

JISBELLA: No.

PRIME MINISTER: On behalf of the federal government, you're welcome. People don't want to be left alone. People want a functioning society, with things working the way they should and hamburgers that don't kill people. I spent a long time studying economics. I learned that government is the only thing standing between you and money using you. You know what money doesn't give a shit about?

JISBELLA: What.

PRIME MINISTER: Anything. And left alone, money is the biggest threat to your ability to be self-reliant. And I say that as someone who believes wholeheartedly in free markets. That realization led to the welfare state. The intention was to free people, to whatever extent possible, from the cold, indifferent grip of money.

JISBELLA: Why do you sound like some sort of socialist right now?

PRIME MINISTER: Because they identified the problem correctly. The trouble comes when you try to work out how to fix the problem. For example, we said: freedom from hunger is a right in a rich society. Which by itself is a great notion. But addressing that problem legislatively leads to two groups of people: clients and administrators. And the creation of those two groups, borne of our desire to do good, makes a problem as bad as the original one.

Start with the administrator: his work is to feed the hungry. But if he successfully feeds the hungry, his work ends and he's out of a job. So he has to constantly change the definition of hunger. Changing the definition goes by another name in bureaucratic circles: raising standards.

Now, the clients. The problem there is that—

JISBELLA: Is that people cheat the system, take advantage of it.

PRIME MINISTER: No. The number of people who abuse the system is statistically insignificant.

On the client side, the problem is this: once a right has been achieved, it's taken for granted. You're a great example of this. A single mother who's had multiple state-sponsored abortions and is now a member of parliament. A couple of generations ago, that sentence would have seemed bizarre. But do you get up every morning and count the ways women have advanced in the last fifty years?

JISBELLA: *(laughs)* Right! I spend all day trying to get you guys to stop looking at my tits when I'm making a point.

PRIME MINISTER: Yes. So—

JISBELLA: Not you, by the way.

PRIME MINISTER: I—

JISBELLA: You never get distracted by the girls.

PRIME MINISTER: Um.

JISBELLA: I'm saying: I've never caught you looking at my breasts.

PRIME MINISTER: Well.

JISBELLA: It's a bit insulting, actually. Are they no good?

PRIME MINISTER: No, I'm just, I—

JISBELLA: Are you too good for them?

PRIME MINISTER: What?

JISBELLA: Too good for my breasts.

PRIME MINISTER: I—

JISBELLA: Look at them.

PRIME MINISTER: What?

JISBELLA: Look at my breasts. Look at them.

PRIME MINISTER: Well, no.

JISBELLA: Jesus. You're too good for my breasts!

PRIME MINISTER: No, I, listen, what I wanted to—

JISBELLA: No. Stop. Stop.

A beat.

Look at them.

A beat. Grimly, slowly, he moves his eyes from hers down to her chest. After a pause, he raises them again.

Nice. Okay.

PRIME MINISTER: Okay.

A beat.

So, the point is, the client group takes for granted every freedom. And naturally it looks for the next one it needs to acquire. This is good. It's human nature, and it's good. You stand at the pinnacle of achievement for a woman in this society, and your next goal is to get men to stop objectifying you. Now, on—

JISBELLA: Sometimes.

PRIME MINISTER: …Right. So, you've got clients who believe it's their right to be free from hunger, and administrators who are constantly changing the definition of hunger. And politicians get elected by saying yes to this cycle of assumed rights and rising standards. But if you say no to that cycle, then you get accused of lowering standards and taking away people's rights.

JISBELLA: So that's you? You're the guy who finally says no? You're the guy nobody wants to be?

PRIME MINISTER: That's my persona, yes. But my real purpose—I didn't get into politics because I looked around and decided to be the hatchet. I'm not a sadist. I'm here for the same reason you are, as it turns out: I want to defend, to revive the notion of self-reliance.

JISBELLA: I knew it!

PRIME MINISTER: What.

JISBELLA: You and me, we are the same. We have the same ideas. Isn't it weird, you can always sense when you're with someone who's basically the same as you, even if he comes off like a complete motherfucking asshole!

PRIME MINISTER: Like I said, that's just my persona.

JISBELLA: Sorry.

PRIME MINISTER: No no. And you know what? You're right. We are the same.

A beat between them.

Anyway. You try to solve one economic problem, you create a half-dozen that are based in human nature. And human nature, Ms. Lyth, is way more complicated than economics.

JISBELLA: That's funny. You're still scared of my first name. Can I get you another?

PRIME MINISTER: No, I'm fine. Sorry, I should have offered you more Scotch.

JISBELLA: That's okay. I'm self-reliant. Keep going.

She crosses to the credenza, gets another drink.

PRIME MINISTER: Leo Strauss, one of the guys I mentioned, talked about two kinds of nihilism. Do you know what that is?

JISBELLA: Nihilism? Like, fuck all this shit?

PRIME MINISTER: A, yes, an absence of prevailing values, leading to the sense that life is meaningless.

JISBELLA: Fuck, all this shit is fucked.

PRIME MINISTER: Yes. One kind of nihilism leads to fascism, the other kind, which is the kind he feels we have in Western society, is a kind of gentler version. A permissive kind of egalitarian everybody's-ideas-count-kind-of situation. The biggest problem with the client and the administrator?

JISBELLA: *(returning)* Yeah?

PRIME MINISTER: Both are Canadian. So the transaction between them is going to be polite. It's going to be, above all other things, non-judgmental. It's going to be: However you got in this situation and became a client of the state, it's okay, I'm not going to judge you. We are equal.

JISBELLA: What's wrong with that?

PRIME MINISTER: Well, it's not true. The exact opposite is true—they are, in that moment, completely unequal. But agreeing not to pass judgment means you're not even allowed to examine what might be wrong with that situation. Judgment is necessary.

JISBELLA: You think we should wander around judging each other all the time?

PRIME MINISTER: I think that if ideas aren't allowed to compete, then we risk that nihilism Strauss talked about.

JISBELLA: It sounds like you're just afraid of the mess.

PRIME MINISTER: How do you mean?

JISBELLA: Well, I have my ideas. What if I don't want them to compete with yours? I just want to have my ideas. What you don't like is everyone walking around thinking whatever they think, no matter how stupid what they think is. What you call nihilism is actually just free people being free. Which is messy as fuck.

PRIME MINISTER: I have no interest in controlling what people think.

JISBELLA: That's not what I said. What I said was: Does the idea that people are walking around thinking whatever they want, the mess of that, does that make you nervous?

PRIME MINISTER: People, I admit it, make me… people are not my strong suit.

JISBELLA: No shit. You're the nerdiest prime minister in the history of Canada. You're like a box of mashed potatoes in a suit.

PRIME MINISTER: Yes, but I feel I've come some distance in that regard.

JISBELLA: I read a thing where some guy asks you if you love this country, and you say, what did you say, you said, like: "Well, it's okay, you know, pretty good, you know."

PRIME MINISTER: Oh, God, I know. But who's ready for that question?

JISBELLA: "It's okay, it'll do, in my opinion."

PRIME MINISTER: It was the start of a campaign, and we had been working hard for weeks on the issues, and this, this, this *guy*—

JISBELLA: "It's a little fat, a little fucking ugly, but I guess I could dance with it."

PRIME MINISTER: And I just: there's always a dozen things that fly through your mind. Especially with the tricky questions.

JISBELLA: How is that question tricky?

PRIME MINISTER: But I'm never going to say the easy, stupid, moronic thing, you know?

JISBELLA: What. That you do in fact love the country you're trying to run?

PRIME MINISTER: I didn't think of it in those terms. I didn't get into this because of love; I mean, I saw very clearly that there's a job to do. I saw very clearly that I could do that job, and nobody else qualified was around to do it. I saw it in those terms.

JISBELLA: You basically said: "I can make this place my bitch."

PRIME MINISTER: I believe I said a lot of stuff, and then just gave up and said the country has a lot of potential.

JISBELLA: "She's fuckable, but not dateable."

PRIME MINISTER: I know, I know.

A pause. She rises.

JISBELLA: One more?

PRIME MINISTER: I'm good. You go ahead.

She pours herself a Scotch.

I could answer it now, though.

JISBELLA: Oh yeah?

PRIME MINISTER: Because when I was asked that fucking moronic question, I had yet to go to the North. Have you been up there?

JISBELLA: I spent a month in Sudbury one weekend.

PRIME MINISTER: It's incredible. It's big, actually big. And just completely empty. I just, I relax when I go north. And under it all, all this emptiness, is a richness. Twenty-five per cent of the world's oil and gas. Buried, out of reach, too expensive to extract, ours but not ours, you know?

JISBELLA: Social retard likes the isolation.

PRIME MINISTER: That is... an acute observation.

A pause.

> Oh, by the way, we're going to let your abortion bill get to second reading.

JISBELLA: Why?

PRIME MINISTER: Well, it seems the airplanes we're committed to are going to be a little more expensive than we thought.

JISBELLA: How much more?

PRIME MINISTER: Nobody can tell me. So when that hits, I'll need you to pop up again. That means you'll have to defend your bill at committee.

JISBELLA: Okay.

PRIME MINISTER: And possibly also debate it in the House.

JISBELLA: Okay. There's still no chance of this thing passing, though, is there?

PRIME MINISTER: No chance at all.

JISBELLA: Okay. Good.

A pause.

PRIME MINISTER: Maybe we should call it a—

JISBELLA: So, why are you doing this?

PRIME MINISTER: Which?

JISBELLA: Why is a social retard putting himself through the endless bullshit of politics? Is there a goal, an end point?

PRIME MINISTER: Oh yes.

JISBELLA: You won't be one of those guys, hang on to power for as long as possible?

PRIME MINISTER: Nope.

JISBELLA: So what's the goal?

PRIME MINISTER: The goal is so simple. It's a number. It's—.

No, you know what, first, I'm going to tell you what my goals aren't. I'm going to list the things I don't believe in, okay?

JISBELLA: You might need another drink for that.

PRIME MINISTER: No, I'm— Oh, what the hell.

During the following, he crosses to the credenza and pours more Scotch in his glass. He then crosses to her, refills her glass, and returns to the desk. His glass remains on the credenza. She clocks this.

Okay. I don't believe in abortion. By which I mean, I don't care about it as an issue. I have personal feelings about it, tied up in my faith, but I don't care about it as your prime minister. See the distinction?

JISBELLA: Uh huh.

PRIME MINISTER: I don't care about Quebec. At all. I am indifferent to its endless quest for whatever it is that it's searching for. I don't care about gay marriage. I don't care about gun laws or building prisons, or the British monarchy. I have nothing against artists, or the CBC. I don't care about hospital wait times. I don't care about the United Nations. I don't care about Western alienation, a thing I'm renowned for caring about. I don't care about whether or not we conduct a national long-form census. I don't give a shit how a scientist spends his time, or who pays him for it. I don't care about which drugs are criminalized or decriminalized. I, oh, GOD, I DO NOT CARE ABOUT THE MOTHERFUCKING SENATE. I don't care if they build a walkway between the shore and the airport in Toronto. I have nothing against David Suzuki. I don't care if the world sees us as peacekeepers or badasses.

(whispering) I don't care about Israel.

(full voice again) I don't care about how much our wheat sells for. I don't care if the pipeline we build goes south to the States or all the way to China. I don't care if our new ships get made in Vancouver or Halifax. I don't care about Nickelback. You know the huge debate about whether human rights tribunals preserve freedoms or inhibit them?

JISBELLA: *(She doesn't.)* Yes.

PRIME MINISTER: I don't care. I don't care about where the salmon went, or why they came back. I don't care about multiculturalism. I don't care if you leave this country for forty years and then come back and try to run it. I don't care how your political party is funded. I don't care about the price of gas. I don't care who tortured whom in Afghanistan, or for what reasons. I don't care who the president of the United States is, and I don't care about whether somebody's kid plays hockey or the accordion. I. Don't. Care.

JISBELLA: I am so hot for you right now.

PRIME MINISTER: What I do care about is this: I want an appropriately sized government.

JISBELLA: A smaller government.

PRIME MINISTER: That's the wrong way to look at it. A government can be as large as it likes, as long as its size is appropriate to the country it serves. Our government is just a little too large to be supported by the country. Just a little. What I want to do is restrict the rate of the government's growth by a few percentage points per year. That's it.

JISBELLA: That's it?

PRIME MINISTER: That's my whole thing. Then I'm outta here.

JISBELLA: That doesn't seem like much of a goal.

PRIME MINISTER: I know. But you know what: it's like the country is a kitten, and I keep saying I want to punch it in the face. When I started in politics, I found out that proposing to nudge us a tiny bit—a tiny bit!—towards being more self-reliant was going to turn me into the very devil.

I don't really think we are in danger of descending into nihilism. I don't think we are in danger of being overwhelmed by the welfare state. I'm just suggesting that we can actually be happier if we move away from those things a tiny bit. And slowly, incrementally, under the cover of all those other things people assume I care about, that's what I'm doing.

JISBELLA: It's a number?

PRIME MINISTER: Sorry?

JISBELLA: You said it's a number?

PRIME MINISTER: Yes! That's the beauty. It's a number, and when I hit it, and set in place a few controls to keep us on that number, then I'm done. The debt-to-GDP ratio. The amount of federal debt relative to how rich we are as a nation. Depending on who you talk to, the number is right now at about 30%. I want to get it to about 22% and keep it there.

JISBELLA: What about just getting rid of debt altogether?

PRIME MINISTER: Debt is very useful. We are part of a world of debt— when countries finance a portion of each other's debt, we remain interconnected in some very useful ways. But reduce that magic number from thirty to twenty-two and something incredible happens.

JISBELLA: What.

PRIME MINISTER: We get happier. We get *happier*. Think of it: tighten things up just a little bit, and suddenly you have to make a few more choices. Fund this initiative, not this one. Do this instead of that. Debate becomes important again, people become engaged politically. And when people become more engaged about anything, life has more meaning, and a life with more meaning is a happier life. But for some reason, when I tell people this, what they hear is—

JISBELLA: "People of earth. Your days are numbered."

PRIME MINISTER: Exactly. I was the only person suggesting this, when I got into politics. None of the parties, Liberal, NDP, Conservative, none of them had any interest in an appropriately sized government. The Conservatives? Not actually conservative. That's why I got into this, and that's also why it's been so easy for everyone to make me look evil. And oh boy, were they good at it. Marketing is a very effective force, Jisbella. I've been made to seem like something I'm not from day one.

And so I had to win people over, slowly, slowly, slowly. I had to build a coalition among the people in the nation I could reach. Some people I will never reach—those who feel that our only purpose is to find more and better ways to express our equality, at whatever cost. I will never make sense to those people, and I don't try to. The ones I can reach are the dissatisfied. Fortunately, there are a great number of dissatisfied people in this country.

That list of things I said I don't care about? All things I have to show some passing interest in in order to build this coalition. And slowly, we did it. I got PCs and Reform together, I got fiscal and social conservatives together, I got Christians and atheists into the same tent. I proved to immigrants that we had their interests at heart, I convinced money and farmers and working-class people that we are their party. And it worked. We wiped them all out. All of them. Incrementally, we changed the face of politics in this country, and incrementally we will change the one tiny thing I want to change. And you know what? I will be loathed while I do it, and I don't care.

A pause.

Sorry, I get going, and then I just… keep going.

JISBELLA: No no. I liked it.

A pause. She's looking at him.

What?

PRIME MINISTER: What? Nothing. What.

JISBELLA: You forgot your drink over there.

PRIME MINISTER: I know. I didn't want it. I wanted you to feel comfortable having a drink.

JISBELLA: So you didn't... huh.

PRIME MINISTER: What.

JISBELLA: I thought. I thought you had a plan. You leave the drink over there, then, at some later point, you realize it's over there, and you get up to get it, and that's when... you make your move.

PRIME MINISTER: I make my move?

JISBELLA: Yes. Isn't that what this is?

A beat.

PRIME MINISTER: No, that's not what this is.

JISBELLA: It's not?

PRIME MINISTER: No.

JISBELLA: Wasn't this, didn't we just... wasn't there something happening here?

PRIME MINISTER: I thought so. I'm glad you came in.

JISBELLA: But, so, why do that if we're not going to have sex?

He has no answer.

You can't treat people like this.

He's silent.

If anybody knew we were here, they'd assume that's what's happening.

A pause.

I mean, I'm not crazy. Tell me I'm not crazy. Tell me you've at least thought about it.

A pause. She rises.

Wow. Okay.

She goes. She returns.

Can I ask you something? How did you know how many abortions I've had?

PRIME MINISTER: I don't know. It was in the file.

JISBELLA: Huh.

A pause. She looks at him. She might make a move towards him. Almost imperceptibly, he shakes his head. This stops her.

Huh.

She goes. After a beat he rises, puts the bottle back in the credenza. He takes the two glasses, tries to decide what to do about them. He finally puts them in a garbage can. He leaves. He returns. He takes the bag containing the glasses out of the garbage can and leaves with the bag.

Blackout.

SCENE 5A.

JAKE sits patiently. He hears someone through the earpiece.

JAKE: Hi. Yes.

Hello, Mr. Solomon. Nice to meet you, sort of.

Evan, okay. Nice to meet you.

Sorry?

Yes. I'm twenty-five. Yes.

That's right.

That's right. Cormier–Lac-Poule.

Yes.

No, not at all. Happy to answer questions about the prime minister. That's why I'm here.

And is there… I mean, can you see me? Is that the camera? Will there be a cameraman?

Really? Robotically? Okay.

Will there be someone else here to tell me when we're going to start?

Okay. Wow.

No, I just—I mean, when I was let in, I noticed that this whole building seems to be more or less empty. The cuts have been effective, haven't they?

(He laughs.) Yeah.

Okay. I'll… be here.

He waits. The lights fade on him.

Blackout.

SCENE 6.

The PM and CARY.

CARY: The problem is this: we've replaced all the Canadian artwork in our embassies abroad with pictures of the queen.

PRIME MINISTER: How is that a problem?

CARY: Well, now we have all these paintings. Some are old, some are expensive. We have to store them somewhere. And insure them.

PRIME MINISTER: Sell them. Where's Kenney on the immigration bill?

CARY: He hasn't even tabled it yet and people have problems with it.

PRIME MINISTER: The press?

CARY: Worse. The immigration industry has problems with it.

PRIME MINISTER: Them we need. Okay, have him put this into the bill: if you come here on a boat, you sit in jail for a year without a hearing.

CARY: *(laughing)* What?

PRIME MINISTER: Yeah. No due process, no nothing.

CARY: Everyone will freak out!

PRIME MINISTER: Exactly. Then he withdraws that part, says he's sorry, leaves the rest of it, and everybody says: Well, could have been worse. What's next?

CARY: Louise Arbour. She praised the human-rights charter the Arabs came up with.

PRIME MINISTER: Yeah. I'm on it already. Vic Toews is going to stand up in parliament and call her a national disgrace.

CARY: Really? You don't think we'd benefit by doing something a little more nuanced here? Former Supreme Court Justice, UN High Commissioner?

PRIME MINISTER: People who care about Israel don't care about her resumé.

CARY: Got it. The attack ads on Justin Trudeau are done.

PRIME MINISTER: I imagine they practically wrote themselves.

CARY: Ohh yes. They're brutal.

PRIME MINISTER: Yeah, I'm worried about that. If the ads are too successful and he gets into trouble, we'll have to pull them. What else?

CARY: Let's see…

JISBELLA enters, waits.

PRIME MINISTER: Where are we on the Court Challenges Program?

CARY: By December it'll be dead for everyone except linguistic minori-
ties. I still say we should do away with it altogether.

PRIME MINISTER: Well, me too. But *c'est la vie*.

JISBELLA: The Court Challenges Program. What is that?

CARY: Hey, Bella.

PRIME MINISTER: Ms. Lyth. Thanks for coming in. It's a program whereby
the federal government pays people to sue the federal government
over the Charter. An example of the contortions we get into to
make sure everyone's equal in this society. You did very well at
committee, I understand.

JISBELLA: Yeah. It was fun.

PRIME MINISTER: You've done very well out of this bill, as have we. But
I guess now is the time to withdraw it.

JISBELLA: I'd prefer if we didn't.

PRIME MINISTER: Nonetheless.

(turning to CARY) Now—

JISBELLA: I think I have the votes.

A beat.

PRIME MINISTER: I'm sure you don't, but we're not having a vote. Do I have to explain this to you?

CARY: Maybe let's meet in my office later to discuss this. We're in the middle of something here.

JISBELLA: No.

A pause.

PRIME MINISTER: Ms. Lyth—

JISBELLA: Getting this through parliament would be fantastic for me.

PRIME MINISTER: That's no reason to enact a law, because it'd be fun for you.

JISBELLA: Not fun for me, good for me.

PRIME MINISTER: My point stands. The government isn't here to further your unlikely career.

JISBELLA: Just yours?

CARY: Hey!

JISBELLA: I mean it, why can't I use parliament like you do?

PRIME MINISTER: Well, for one thing, because you're not me. For another, YOU'RE NOT ME.

JISBELLA: And thank fuck for that—

CARY: Okay! Let's—

PRIME MINISTER: The fucking bill doesn't even make sense. Criminalizing abortion after twenty weeks? Ninety-five per cent of them happen before twenty weeks. And if you excuse the women that have them after twenty weeks for medical reasons, *which your bill does*, that's the other 5%. Your bill criminalizes a problem that doesn't exist.

JISBELLA: It's an abortion bill. I'm coming to understand how many people, how much of your base, would like to see one.

PRIME MINISTER: I'm keenly aware of how much the base would like one. The thing you don't get is how many people like things the way they are. My job is to balance the interests of all those people.

JISBELLA: Well, it's not mine.

PRIME MINISTER: Fuck me, what have we created here? Listen. The abortion debate in this country is closed, as of right now.

JISBELLA: Why do you insist on misunderestimating me?

PRIME MINISTER: Is that what I do?

CARY: Hey! Enough! We don't have time to for this right now.

JISBELLA: YOU KNOW WHAT?

She stops herself.

No. Okay.

She goes.

CARY: Incredible.

PRIME MINISTER: Does she have the votes?

CARY: No.

PRIME MINISTER: Are you absolutely certain?

CARY: No.

PRIME MINISTER: Fuck me.

A pause.

CARY: Remember at the start of all this, how she said we faked the signature on her nomination papers?

PRIME MINISTER: Yeah.

CARY: She made it up. She signed them.

PRIME MINISTER: She made that up? All the rotten borough stuff?

CARY: On the fly. Yup.

PRIME MINISTER: How do you like that? We've been misunderestimating her. How do you know this?

CARY: I'm sleeping with her.

PRIME MINISTER: You are?

CARY: I thought you knew.

PRIME MINISTER: Why would I know that?

CARY: You know everything.

PRIME MINISTER: Well, then, can you tell her to cut this shit out?

CARY: I've tried. Turns out I'm just sleeping with her.

A pause.

PRIME MINISTER: You know why she's doing this? Because I got into this whole thing where—

CARY: 'Cause you wouldn't have sex with her?

PRIME MINISTER: She told you that?

CARY *shrugs.*

>She misread the situation.

CARY: Are you sure?

A beat.

>Anyway, you know how you fix it?

PRIME MINISTER: I'm not doing it.

CARY: She looks up to you. She talks about you all the time.

PRIME MINISTER: I'm not going to have sex with that woman.

CARY: I'd be cool with it, if that's what you're worried about.

PRIME MINISTER: No! That's—

CARY: Here, let me help: I quit.

PRIME MINISTER: What?!

CARY: Sure. Sleeping with her fixes your problem, having me around after is going to be too awkward for you, so: I quit.

PRIME MINISTER: You can't quit!

CARY: Of course I can. You're the only one in this for the long haul.

PRIME MINISTER: But what will you do?

CARY: Are you kidding? I get ten calls a week from the private sector wondering when I'm going to get out of politics and do something with my life.

PRIME MINISTER: But—

CARY: Nothing happens when there's a crisis except for work on the crisis. Fix your crisis.

Blackout.

SCENE 6A.

A red light comes on. JAKE sits up, clears his throat.

JAKE: Hello, Evan. It's, I'm a pleasure to be here.

Yes, twenty-five, that's right.

Yes, that's right. I'll be running in Cormier–Lac-Poule. I moved back to the riding after university.

Yes. I was seven or eight when my mother entered politics, and I was fourteen when she quit. She says hello, by the way.

He laughs.

Well, thanks. I know she'd take that as a compliment. She always enjoys appearing on your show. Since leaving politics and becoming a lobbyist she's made a career out of having strong opinions.

She finds it ridiculous, to be honest, the fact I'm not running as a Conservative. Especially in a riding that she turned Conservative and that the Conservatives have held since then. Not that she's hurt by my decision, she just finds it idiotic. She says I always find the hardest way of doing something.

Which is why I want to be very careful about this. I have this connection with the prime minister, and I want to make sure that my respect for him and for what he did for me and my mother remains the headline. Prime Minister Harper was a big presence in my life during the years my mother was in politics. He was in some ways a surrogate father. When I started showing an interest in politics, he and I had long talks. He was always very generous with me in that way. When I announced at the age of eleven that I wanted to get an economics degree, he was so excited he sent a cake to our house.

I know. Not exactly the image people have of him. He was a lot more excited about it than my mother was, let me tell you.

During the following, the PRIME MINISTER enters his office, and, after looking around, goes to the credenza and pours some Scotch.

I agree. My mother was ahead of her time. She accomplished a lot during her six years in Ottawa. And people forget, when she started out, it was just a job to her. A much better job than the one she had.

That's right, managing a St-Hubert. One day she pulls me out of school, says to me: "Pack up, Jakie, we're going to Ottawa. I got a government job."

I agree with that. She was a radical, in her way. Take her first private member's bill, before she was in cabinet, the abortion bill. The last thing the prime minister wanted to do was reopen the abortion debate, and he had the hardest time killing it. He always said that he went to extraordinary lengths to change my mother's mind on that abortion law. *She* always said that tabling that bill was the most fun she ever had in politics.

JISBELLA enters the PRIME MINISTER's *office, stands in the doorway. The lights fade on* JAKE.

SCENE 7.

JISBELLA: Hi.

PRIME MINISTER: Hello.

JISBELLA: Do you have a condom?

PRIME MINISTER: Yes. Yes I do.

A beat.

Would you like a…

He starts to search for a second glass.

JISBELLA: Sure.

He searches.

You know what I've never understood?

PRIME MINISTER: What's that?

JISBELLA: Scotch. It tastes bad. It's just bad-tasting. It's like it was invented to remind you you have a hard life. The taste of Scotch says: Your life is shitty, it sucks, it'll never get better. And now you're drunk, so go to bed.

PRIME MINISTER: I can't, there only seems to be one glass.

JISBELLA: That's okay.

He pours Scotch, crosses down to her, hands her the glass. She drinks. He takes the glass, returns to the credenza, pours, then crosses to her again. He is about to drink when she takes the glass out of his hand. She puts it on the desk. He sighs deeply. She steps in. She waits. A pause. It grows. It grows past the sexy point and enters an awkward phase.

What has to happen is, you have to let the gnawing hunger you have for me overwhelm any reservations you're having.

PRIME MINISTER: I know, I know.

JISBELLA: You have to let the thing inside you that got you this far—unleash that, let it, just, you know, let it go.

PRIME MINISTER: Okay.

JISBELLA: Let it out.

PRIME MINISTER: Yes.

JISBELLA: Unleash the beast, sir.

PRIME MINISTER: Yup.

Another pause. She takes his hand, puts it under her blouse.

Yup.

A beat.

What is *wrong* with me?

JISBELLA: I'll tell you exactly what's wrong with you. No no, don't go anywhere. What's wrong with you is, you're treating this like it means something. But it doesn't. It's just a thing.

PRIME MINISTER: That's right.

JISBELLA: Pretend it's, I don't know, like the United Nations. Meaningless.

PRIME MINISTER: Okay.

She moves in, incrementally, and kisses him.

Mmm. Mm hmm. Or NATO.

JISBELLA: That's right.

More kissing.

PRIME MINISTER: Consequences later, right now, the, this part.

JISBELLA: Yes.

PRIME MINISTER: This kind of thing goes on all the time, everywhere—

JISBELLA: Yes—

PRIME MINISTER: People just, unhinging their brains—

JISBELLA: Letting go—

PRIME MINISTER: Letting go of… themselves—

JISBELLA: Themselves—

PRIME MINISTER: Or meaning, or a point, or—

JISBELLA: Uh huh—

PRIME MINISTER: It's just pointless, stupid, stupid…

They've stopped.

 Stupid. Fun.

 What.

JISBELLA: Um.

PRIME MINISTER: No, c'mon, I want this. I want to be just like people.

He moves towards her. Kisses her.

 And you'll…

JISBELLA: Yes?

PRIME MINISTER: After this, you'll…

JISBELLA: Yes?

PRIME MINISTER: You'll drop the whole abortion… thing?

JISBELLA: Mmmm.

PRIME MINISTER: Mmmm?

JISBELLA: Mmmm. No.

He breaks away.

PRIME MINISTER: No?

JISBELLA: Of course not. Don't be stupid.

PRIME MINISTER: Then why am I doing this?

JISBELLA: ARE YOU KIDDING ME?

PRIME MINISTER: That's what this is. We have sex, and because of the sex, you drop the bill.

JISBELLA: What are you, fourteen?

PRIME MINISTER: Cary said it would work.

JISBELLA: Cary's a moron!

PRIME MINISTER: It's either this or I have to destroy you.

JISBELLA: Unmaking me is going to be a lot tougher than it was making me. You really think you can destroy me?

PRIME MINISTER: I think, if I wanted to, I could have you back working the fucking midnight shift at St-Hubert in a week.

She advances on him.

JISBELLA: Two things: First, I find it unbearably hot when you speak to me like that. Second, I'm going to do you a favour.

PRIME MINISTER: What's that.

JISBELLA: I'm going to have sex with you. Right here, right now.

PRIME MINISTER: No you're not.

JISBELLA: Yes I am. You know why?

PRIME MINISTER: No.

JISBELLA: Because you want it.

PRIME MINISTER: No I don't.

JISBELLA: Yes you do. I've seen it: you want it. You don't want to want it, but you want it. And after that, you know what we're gonna do?

PRIME MINISTER: What.

JISBELLA: We're gonna have sex again. And after that, you know what's gonna happen?

PRIME MINISTER: More sex?

JISBELLA: No. After that, you are going to publicly endorse the abortion bill I'm going to get through parliament.

PRIME MINISTER: Who are you.

JISBELLA: You'll endorse it because, like you said, it criminalizes a problem that doesn't exist. It changes nothing for the people that want things to stay the same, but the base finally gets an abortion bill. It works *because* it's meaningless. It's perfect politics.

PRIME MINISTER: You— That's actually not bad.

JISBELLA: *(advancing)* Great. Now, let's take care of this other thing.

The PM rounds the desk.

PRIME MINISTER: No, look: stop.

A pause. They look at each other. He looks down.

Okay. Yes. I want you.

JISBELLA: Yes.

PRIME MINISTER: Yes. Fine. I do. I fantasize about you all the time.

JISBELLA: That's right.

PRIME MINISTER: Yes. I fantasize about bringing you into cabinet. You're going to be the human face of this government. And together we're gonna bring peace and prosperity and long-term, boring, stable happiness to this country. That's what I fantasize about.

JISBELLA: That's the sickest fucking fantasy I've ever heard. Shut up and get over here!

CARY appears at the door, condoms in hand.

CARY: Hi guys. Just thought I'd drop by some condoms, in case, you know…

JISBELLA: Get out of here!

PRIME MINISTER: Help me!

SCENE 8.

Lights up on JAKE.

JAKE: I owe my mother everything. Everything. When I think of the things she did, the places she bullied her way into so that she could take care of us, her and me, her little family… She was sick a few years ago, as I'm sure you know, and when she needed a new liver, I gave her part of mine. And she, I mean, *(He smiles again.)* my mother used to go on and on about the importance of self-reliance. But now that she's walking around with someone else's liver, she doesn't really talk about self-reliance any more. I think she's been shown the limits of the concept.

That's right. The fact we disagree politically is… immaterial. The bond goes deeper than politics. My decision to run as an independent is a disappointment to her, but in the end, I'm still her kid.

Well, I'm running as an independent because ever since the Liberals, the NDP, and the Greens became a single party, I've found our politics have become over-simple. I understand why the left felt it had to unite to seek power. Maybe it was inevitable. But here's the thing: Mr. Harper is the country's longest-serving prime minister at this point. And whether he intended to or not, Mr. Harper created a binary state: for us or against us. Which is an incredibly efficient way to conduct politics. It's rational. But I think that it's a terrible way to serve a country as large and diverse as Canada.

Oh, he and I have been arguing about the binary state since I was seventeen. He loves to get into that stuff. He says that ideas have to compete to become real. Say whatever else you want about him, Mr. Harper has sharpened the debate around here.

I can't entirely disagree: there has been *economic* stability. But, and I say this with all due respect, that's the easiest part of the job. He presides over a resource economy, and the world is clamouring for our resources. But a moment will come when the resource economy will be all gone. The North is being ripped open—there's no other word for it, ripped open—and drained, and someday those who are doing the draining will leave. At that point, what will bind us? At that point, what will keep the politics of the binary from ripping *us* open, ripping us apart?

A beat.

You know, Mr. Harper always said to me: We will have stability. We will have security. It'll be long-term and boring, but it will be stability. And that will bring us happiness. And I guess I feel...

A pause.

I guess I feel like that's the wrong thing to want.

We are enormously lucky to live here. And the way we honour our good luck is not by simplifying things, but by asking more of ourselves. I love this country and I think our obligation to it never ends. It certainly doesn't end with our being happy.

Well, speaking personally, I think the only thing we can consistently say about our politics is that they cycle between strength and decline and renewal. So we try, and mostly fail, and try some more, and mostly fail, and try again, mostly fail, and that seems to be the pattern. But we only fail mostly, not completely. And in the little successes we... advance.

There are those who say that our successes don't need to be small, that they can be complete. They say that the solutions are simple, if only to them. They miss the point of our project, of this country: we are meant simply to wear ourselves out. Wear ourselves out making something so complicated it's impossible to see in its totality. It's something so big, so difficult, it is in its truest sense a shared thing. And my life to this point has taught me one thing: we are meant to do that, as best we can, together.

Well, thank you very much, Evan. Wish me luck.

After a moment, the red light goes out. He stands and begins the complicated act of microphone removal. The lights fade on him as he does this.

Blackout.

End of play.

photo © John Healey

Michael Healey is an actor and playwright. He performed in his first one-act play in 1996 as part of the Fringe Festival of Toronto. Since then he has become one of the exceptional voices in Canadian theatre. With an outstanding breadth of work, Michael has won a number of awards as a playwright, including the Dora Mavor Moore Award, the Governor General's Literary Award, and the Chalmers Canadian Play Award. He lives in Toronto.